Acting Out Matthew's Message

Lenten Dialogues Exploring the Gospel of Matthew

Roger E. Timm

CSS Publishing Company, Inc.
Lima, Ohio

Reviews for *Acting Out Matthew's Message*

The penitential season of Lent invites Christians to devote themselves to diligent biblical study, persistent prayer, honest self-reflection, sincere repentance, and faithful service. In this volume, Timm offers his readers fifteen dialogues that are organized into three distinct series. The dialogues present a variety of vignettes describing common life experiences and reflecting on those experiences in light of specific Matthean passages. Human stories are creatively interwoven with the biblical message and the tapestry that the author creates serves as a thoughtful and incisive spiritual guide for an individual Christian's or a Christian community's Lenten journey. However, the usefulness and applicability of these materials are not limited to the season of Lent. Since they do not focus specifically on the passion narrative but explore other sections of Matthew, they can serve as a welcome devotional resource throughout the church year. The author's biblical interpretations are carefully nuanced, his theological insights are intentionally relevant to faithful Christian living, and his ethical vision is both challenging and encouraging. All of the materials reflect pastoral sensitivity and integrity. While the dialogues were originally created for the liturgical setting of midweek Lenten services, for which they are well-suited, they could also be used efficaciously in personal devotions, individual or corporate Bible study, spiritual retreats, and adult forums. This small volume is surely a welcome spiritual resource for both pastors and lay people.

Kurt K. Hendel
Bernard, Fischer, Westberg Distinguished Ministry Professor
    of Reformation History
Lutheran School of Theology at Chicago

Participating in most all of the Lenten dialogues, either as a presenter or an observer, was one of the most meaningful parts of my Lenten discipline. Over each Lenten season, we journeyed along with Matt and his associates. Ordinary events from Matt's (and our) life brought home the gospel's message in a very accessible format — and always left us with something more to think about.

From a performance perspective, the dialogues were easy for the presenters to learn. We had our scripts with us, so memorization was not necessary. There was room for a little bit of improvisation as desired. There was also a freshness each week as a new twosome would present the dialogue, which made it very easy for the congregation to stay engaged and absorb the lesson.

When combined with Holden Evening Prayer, the Lenten services were meditative, thoughtful, beautiful, and calming — all within 30 minutes.

Amy Haara
Member of Ascension Lutheran Church
Riverside, Illinois

Midweek Lenten services are fast becoming a part of worship history. However, there are pastors like Roger Timm who would rather not succumb to that growing trend and instead developed a series of short plays based on Matthew's gospel to be used in midweek Lenten worship. As one who participated in the plays and also was a part of the worshiping congregation I can say that midweek Lenten worship took on a new meditative meaning. Each of the parables took on contemporary meaning as Pastor Timm was able to take ancient words and make them feel as if they were being spoken today.

Any pastor who is looking for something new to be used during midweek Lenten worship cannot go wrong in trying these short plays. As a former bishop I know the struggles that pastors go through trying to keep midweek Lenten worship alive. Acting Out Matthew's Message *will provide that necessary lift.*

Rev. Paul Landahl
Member and former pastor of Ascension Lutheran Church, Riverside, Illinois
Former Bishop, Metropolitan Chicago Synod, ELCA

Table of Contents

Introduction   7

Probing the Parables —
Hearing Their Questions for Us

Week 1: Pearls, Nets, and Treasure Chests   11
    Matthew 13:44-52
Week 2: The Unforgiving Debtor   15
    Matthew 18:21-35
Week 3: Unfair Labor Practices in the Vineyard   20
    Matthew 20:1-16
Week 4: Etiquette for Heavenly Wedding Guests   26
    Matthew 22:1-14
Week 5: The Great Judgment   30
    Matthew 25:31-46

From Discourse to Dialogue —
Sermons From the Five "Books" of Matthew

Week 1: The Sermon on the Mount   37
    Matthew 5:13-30
Week 2: Instructions for Disciples   42
    Matthew 10:5-20
Week 3: Parables of the Kingdom   47
    Matthew 13:10-17, 31-33
Week 4: Instructions for the Church   52
    Matthew 18:1-14
Week 5: Warnings of Final Judgment   57
    Matthew 24:1-35

Mysteries of Matthew:
Proclaiming "Both" to the Gospel's Balancing Act

Week 1: Turning Cheeks or Resisting Evil?   65
    Matthew 5:38-48

Week 2: Don't Worry — Be Faithful Matthew 6:24-34	70
Week 3: Only the Lost Sheep of the House of Israel? Matthew 15:21-28	75
Week 4: How Often Should We Forgive? Matthew 18:15-35	80
Week 5: Clothes for the Wedding Banquet Matthew 22:1-14	85

Introduction

This book includes three series of Lenten dialogues based on the gospel of Matthew and intended for use during Cycle A of the Revised Common Lectionary. Working with the assumption that Lent is a time for study and reflection and avoiding a focus on the Passion narrative before Holy Week, I wrote each of these series to explore the message of Matthew from a slightly different perspective.

The first series, *Probing the Parables — Hearing Their Questions for Us*, deals with a set of five parables in Matthew's gospel. Each dialogue ends with a question for the hearers' continuing reflection.

The second series, *From Discourse to Dialogue — Sermons from the Five "Books" of Matthew*, is organized on the premise that Matthew intentionally structured his gospel in five sections akin to the five books of Moses. The dialogues explore the message of the discourse found in each of these five sections.

Mysteries of Matthew: Proclaiming "Both" to the Gospel's Balancing Act, the third series, was inspired by noticing how often Matthew seems to want to balance the newness of Jesus' message with its reinforcing of Old Testament faith and practice. Notice the difference between the parable of the banquet in Luke and Matthew; only in Matthew do we hear of the expulsion of the wedding guest who refuses to put on a wedding garment. Each dialogue in this series takes up a different aspect of Matthew's "balancing act," and the characters advocate for each competing emphasis with a final "proclamation" that Matthew intends to affirm both emphases.

These dialogues were used originally within a service of Evening Prayer that was part of a midweek Lenten gathering for a meal and worship. The dialogues could also be used as part of a Sunday worship service, in a retreat setting, or in an adult forum studying the gospel of Matthew.

We kept the setting for the dialogues simple — two chairs in front of the congregation, perhaps with a few props suggested by the specific skit. Such simple staging makes these dialogues usable in many contexts, but more elaborate use of props and stage settings may be helpful in reinforcing the message of each dialogue.

The conversation in these dialogues is intended to be realistic and to express the good-natured banter that might occur between friends or family members. Dialogue participants should be encouraged to emphasize these moments of humor in the script.

A word on the names of the characters: Perhaps it's obvious that "Matt" would be an appropriate name for a male character in a series of dialogues on Matthew. I wanted to choose names unlike anyone in our congregation but that would also have a biblical meaning, so I chose "Lydia." Similarly, I used "Irene" — also because it means "peace." "Angela" became a favorite of mine because of its relation to "angel" and hence to a "messenger." In the third series I wanted to choose names that reflected the tension I was highlighting in Matthew; the two halves of "Matt-hew" suggested the names "Matt" and "Eunice" to me. With the possible exception of the third series, the names are not integral to the message of the skits, and other names surely can be substituted.

Probing the Parables —
Hearing Their Questions for Us

Week 1

Pearls, Nets, and Treasure Chests

Matthew 13:44-52

Matt and Lydia are watching **Antiques Roadshow**.

Lydia: Look at that pearl ring! How beautiful! I'll bet that's worth a lot.

Matt: How do you know? It looks like just an ordinary piece of jewelry to me.

Lydia: Oh no. I can tell that it's worth a lot.

Matt: How can you tell?

Lydia: I just know. I hang around James & Williams,[1] the jewelers, a lot.

Matt: Listen, the appraiser is about to give his estimate.

Lydia: $80,000? He's wrong; that ring is worth a lot more.

Matt: Are you sure? $80,000 seems like a lot of money for a ring to me.

Lydia: Yes, I'm sure. I can tell that that pearl is a lot more special than the appraiser realizes. We've got to buy that ring, Matt.

Matt: How are we going to do that?

Lydia: I don't know — maybe she'll sell the ring on eBay or something.

Matt: That's not exactly what I meant. What I meant was "How are we going to come up with $80,000?"

Lydia: I don't know how, but we have to. I think that pearl is worth over a million dollars.

Matt: A million dollars? That's what you think — without any proof that I can see. You know that our credit cards are maxed out, and we don't have that much in savings.

Lydia: Don't we have an IRA? And there's your 401k plan.

Matt: Yes, but we can't afford the penalty if we withdraw from them before our retirement time.

Lydia: Can we sell our house?

Matt: What, and live on the street? Are you going crazy? We just don't have that much money. What we have is not liquid or we need it for regular expenses. Is this pearl really worth our going deeply in debt, or giving up our most important financial assets?

Lydia: I think so.

Matt: Why?

Lydia: Because that ring is worth at least twenty times as much as the appraiser said.

Matt: So getting something of great financial value is worth creating all this financial chaos in our lives?

Lydia: Hmmm, I didn't think of it that way. Maybe not.

Matt: What *do* you think is worth selling all you have?

Lydia: How about selling all that I have to become president?

Matt: Ah yes, "President Lydia Disciple." That has a certain ring to it. Do you want all the conflict and responsibility that goes with that office?

Lydia: Not really. I'm not sure anything is worth selling all that I have.

Matt: Nothing? How about Jesus?

Lydia: Jesus? Is this Sunday school, where the right answer to everything is always "Jesus"? Jesus. I suppose you're right, though. Knowing the love and forgiveness Jesus brought us is priceless — and ultimately more valuable than anything else I might want to buy with all that I have. But I thought God's love in Christ was free. How would I sell all that I have to buy this pearl of God's love?

Matt: Yes, God's love is a free gift, but God also expects our total commitment in return. God asks us not to sell all that we have but to give all that we are.

Lydia: Can I do this on an installment plan?

Matt: What do you mean?

Lydia: I don't know how to "give all that I am" to God and keep on with my regular daily life. Do I have to become a pastor or a full-time church worker of some kind?

Matt: Not if you really want to buy that pearl ring! Yes, serving full time in the church is one way to "give all that you are," but it's not the only way.

Lydia: Are there other ways to show day by day that I have given my whole self in response to God's love?

Matt:	Sure. "Giving all that you are" doesn't mean "giving up all that you are." In fact, it may mean using the talents and interests that make you who you are to honor God and serve others. Basically it has to do with living your daily life in the spirit of the love we see in Christ.
Lydia:	So I'm supposed to love like Jesus when I cook for our family, change our kid's diapers, and deal with my nasty boss at work?
Matt:	I didn't say it was going to be easy, but yes, loving like Jesus means caring for what's best for others whether they deserve it or not.
Lydia:	What a challenge!
Matt:	Yes, this is the challenge: "How do we show day by day that we have given our whole selves in response to God's love in Christ?"

---

1. A high-quality jewelry store in the author's neighborhood. Substitute an appropriate name from your locale.

Week 2

The Unforgiving Debtor

Matthew 18:21-35

Lydia and her friend Irene are chatting over their morning coffee. The conversation soon turns to Lydia's issue with her husband, Matt.

Lydia: I don't know how I can ever forgive him!

Irene: Forgive whom?

Lydia: Well, Matt, of course.

Irene: Why? What did he do?

Lydia: I can't believe that he'd say something like that! He can be so insensitive!

Irene: Say what? What was so insensitive?

Lydia: It's what he said last night. You know all the clearance sales they've been having recently? Well, I bought a new dress yesterday, and I tried it on to see how it looked on me. I asked him, "Does this dress make me look fat?"

Irene: Oh-oh, I can see the train wreck coming.

Lydia: Well, Matt said, "I like the dress, but it does make you look a little chunky." I can't believe he said that!

Irene: Do you think he was right?

Lydia: Irene, how could you? Are you siding with Matt?

Irene: No, I'm just wondering if he was trying to be honest.

Lydia:	Maybe he was right, but that's no excuse for being insulting!
Irene:	I guess honesty isn't always the best policy — or the best diplomacy. What would it take to help you forgive him?
Lydia:	He could say he was sorry. Flowers and candy wouldn't hurt either.
Irene:	Does he know how upset you are?
Lydia:	Not really. After his little insensitivity I went off to the bedroom and sulked for a while.
Irene:	I see. Well, why don't you tell Matt how you feel to see how he reacts? Maybe he will apologize.
Lydia:	Okay, you're right. And he's usually pretty good about saying he's sorry when he upsets me. He's a lot better than my sister.
Irene:	Your sister?
Lydia:	Yes, my sister.
Irene:	What does your sister do?
Lydia:	She's been cutting me down my whole life.
Irene:	How so?
Lydia:	Let's see. When I was in grade school and I was all excited about a good grade I got, she'd tell my parents that it was an easy test, or that she got a better grade. Or in high school when I told them about my date to the prom, she said what a loser he was. Or my first job — she said what a dead-end job it was. Then when I married Matt, she told my best friend at the reception that she supposed he was okay as a "starter husband."
Irene:	You've got quite a list. I guess you've never heard

about "forgive and forget."

Lydia: What do you mean? Those were really hurtful comments. How am I supposed to forget them?

Irene: Actually, you're right. You may not be able to forget those put-downs. But you could forgive them. Have you ever talked with her about how her comments make you feel?

Lydia: Yes, I have. She just says that I'm too sensitive and that I take her comments too seriously.

Irene: But her comments do hurt you, don't they?

Lydia: Yes, they do. Rightly or wrongly, they bother me.

Irene: When you've tried to tell your sister how you feel, does she say she's sorry?

Lydia: Half-heartedly, I think. She says something like, "Well, if my innocent little teasing bothers you, I guess I'm sorry."

Irene: That is a little half-hearted. Do you think you can forgive her anyway?

Lydia: I'm not sure that I can. If I can't forget and if I can't pretend it doesn't bother me, how can I forgive her?

Irene: Because forgiveness means something else. Forgiveness means letting your anger and resentment go. Forgiveness means not holding something against someone anymore and leaving any kind of judgment up to God.

Lydia: I guess I could forgive in that sense, but why should I?

Irene: That answer is as simple as the Lord's Prayer.

Lydia: What do you mean? Are you getting religious on me?

Irene: Maybe a little! But think of what you say when you pray the Lord's Prayer: "Forgive us our sins, as we forgive those who sin against us." We ask God to forgive us and promise to forgive others in return. If we think about how generous God is in forgiving all our sins and failings, how can we not forgive others?

Lydia: So if God can forgive me, then I should be able to forgive my sister. Is that what you're saying?

Irene: Yes, that's what I'm saying.

Lydia: I see your logic, but I don't think it's that easy. Besides, have I ever hurt God the way my sister has hurt me?

Irene: Isn't that what Good Friday is all about?

Lydia: What do you mean?

Irene: On Good Friday we remember Jesus' crucifixion, but we also say that he died *for us*. We believe that Jesus suffered for our sins too.

Lydia: I know that's what we believe, but I don't think I'm all that sinful. What do I do that's so awful?

Irene: Well, neither of us is an axe murderer, but I know that I'm not as loving and forgiving to others as God has been to me. When I pray the Lord's Prayer, I'm reminded of how much I need God's forgiveness.

Lydia: You're right. I do not love others the way God loves me either. So every time I pray the Lord's Prayer, I suppose the questions are: "Whom do I need to forgive?" and "How can I forgive such a person?"

Irene: Yes, those are the questions: "Whom do I need to forgive?" and "How can I forgive them?"

Week 3

Unfair Labor Practices in the Vineyard

Matthew 20:1-16

Matt and Lydia are talking just after Lydia returns home from choir practice.

Lydia: I am so steamed!

Matt: Why?

Lydia: Irene, our choir director, gave out choir appreciation gifts tonight.

Matt: Why would that upset you? I would think that that would make you happy.

Lydia: Ordinarily it would, but she gave us all the same gift.

Matt: What's wrong with that?

Lydia: It's not fair — that's what's wrong with that!

Matt: I don't understand. How is that unfair?

Lydia: How obtuse can you be, Matt? Isn't it obviously unfair?

Matt: No, not to me. What am I missing? Do you think you should receive something special?

Lydia: As a matter of fact, yes. After all, I've sung in the choir for ten years, and I never miss a rehearsal.

Matt: You don't? What about that time you stayed home to watch an episode of *Downton Abbey*? Or when you went on that shopping trip to the

	outlet mall?
Lydia:	Oh, quiet! Whose side are you on? Besides, that was only a couple times. I'm usually there — and I'm always on time too.
Matt:	*Always* on time? How about —
Lydia:	Okay, *usually* on time. I can't help it if I have to work late sometimes. The point is, I've been exceptionally faithful for ten years, and I get the same award as people who just joined the choir, or as those who regularly miss practices or come late. I think I deserve a special award. It's not fair that I should receive the same as everyone else.
Matt:	Sounds like Sunday school to me.
Lydia:	What do you mean?
Matt:	You remind me of my Sunday school awards for perfect attendance.
Lydia:	That reminds me of something else that bugs me. They don't do that anymore.
Matt:	They don't?
Lydia:	No, instead of giving out awards for perfect attendance in Sunday school, our Education Committee gives out certificates to anyone who attends our Sunday school even once.
Matt:	Really? That's interesting. I guess there just aren't any standards any more.
Lydia:	That's what I think. Even the church isn't fair!
Matt:	But Lydia, I thought you were in the choir because you love to sing.
Lydia:	Yes. So?
Matt:	Well, you've often talked about how you think

	you have a gift for singing and you want to share your ability.
Lydia:	That's true.
Matt:	And you also talk about how much joy you find in the group bonding you've experienced with the choir.
Lydia:	That's true too. Your point?
Matt:	Isn't the joy you have in singing and in being part of the choir reward enough?
Lydia:	I guess so. I surely don't want to give up my singing in the choir. It still doesn't seem fair, though.
Matt:	Maybe it's not about being fair. Maybe Irene is just trying to express her joy over people singing in the choir, whatever their length or level of participation. What about Mary?
Lydia:	What about her?
Matt:	Didn't she just join the choir?
Lydia:	Yes.
Matt:	Didn't you tell me how happy she is to be in the choir — how she's been away from the church for a long time but has never known a church or a choir where she felt so welcomed and accepted?
Lydia:	That's all true, and we all are very happy that Mary is part of the choir now.
Matt:	So maybe Irene gave everyone the same gift because she is just as happy about Mary's newfound joy in being part of the choir as she is about your long and faithful service in the choir.
Lydia:	So Irene doesn't need to be fair when she's trying to express appreciation for each one of us?

Matt: Yes, that's right. That reminds me of one of Jesus' parables.

Lydia: Which one?

Matt: The one where the owner of a vineyard hires workers first thing in the morning and promises to pay them the fair daily wage. He goes back and hires more workers during the day, including at the last hour of the workday. When the day is over, he pays those working the shortest time first and gives them the whole daily wage. When those who worked all day long come to get paid, they expect a larger amount, but the owner gives them the same wage. They complain bitterly that they were treated unfairly.

Lydia: Doesn't the owner say that he was being fair because he gave them what he promised, and besides, can't he do what he wants with his own money?

Matt: Yes, that's right.

Lydia: That parable has always confused me. If the owner of the vineyard is supposed to be God, I don't think God is fair.

Matt: Ahhh, that's the point. By our standards God doesn't always seem fair.

Lydia: But isn't God perfect? If so, shouldn't God be fair?

Matt: God is perfectly loving and perfectly just. God is perfectly fair — by God's standards of fairness.

Lydia: I'm not sure I like God's standards.

Matt: Well, this parable shows that to God, grace and acceptance are more important than what seems fair to us. God rejoices in whoever responds to God's love in faith whenever that occurs. God is just as happy to rejoice in sinners' repenting, whether that happens now or fifty years ago. As the Bible says, "The first shall be last, and the last shall be first."

Lydia: Never mind the choir. Don't I deserve special recognition because I've been a faithful Christian all my life?

Matt: That depends on what you mean by "special." Isn't knowing that you can count on God's love for you pretty special?

Lydia: Yes, but why be a faithful Christian for so long if God gives us love even if we believe only a short time?

Matt: I suppose you have a point, but why wait to be faithful and miss out on all the joy in life that comes from a faithful relationship with God and other Christians?

Lydia: Joy? Isn't working in the vineyard — and in the church — hard work?

Matt: Sure, but working hard and knowing joy in God's presence go together.

Lydia: Perhaps, but there are times when I resent how everyone fawns over those new members who just joined us — as if they were God's gifts!

Matt: Maybe that's exactly what they are — God's gifts to us!

Lydia: You and Jesus! You always have an answer to my complaints. So you're saying that God doesn't always seek fairness, but God does seek to show joy over sinners whenever they repent. So who is

	the last who shall be first? And whom do I need to welcome, no matter how recently they have come to faith?
Matt:	Yes, those are the questions: Who is the last who shall be first? And whom do I need to welcome, no matter how recently they have come to faith?

Week 4

Etiquette for Heavenly Wedding Guests

Matthew 22:1-14

Lydia greets Matt as he returns home from his company's charity golf outing.

Lydia: How did your golf outing go, Matt?

Matt: Oh, pretty well. No holes-in-one, but I had some good drives and I hit par on a couple holes.

Lydia: So did you have a good time?

Matt: Sort of.

Lydia: You don't seem too happy about it. What happened?

Matt: Do you remember how I got invited?

Lydia: Yes, it was something about how most of the top executives couldn't or wouldn't go.

Matt: Right. So a bunch of us new management trainees were invited to go instead. I thought it was kind of cool that we got asked to go instead — a chance for us underlings to enjoy some of the perks of the higher-ups.

Lydia: Isn't that what happened?

Matt: Yes and no. We did get to enjoy the golf outing, but what they didn't tell us — or what I didn't pay attention to — was that all of us who participated got a free round of golf, but at the end we

	were supposed to make a substantial donation to our company's favorite charity.
Lydia:	You didn't know that ahead of time?
Matt:	No, I didn't. They did say it was a charity golf outing, but I never thought that would mean that I'd have to make some big contribution.
Lydia:	I guess there's no free lunch — nor free round of golf! What did you do?
Matt:	Thank God for credit cards! I charged a donation to our MasterCard, but my friend Simon wasn't so lucky.
Lydia:	What do you mean?
Matt:	He didn't have any cash or credit cards with him and he didn't get the message about the donation either, so he refused to make a contribution.
Lydia:	What happened then?
Matt:	His supervisor was there and told him not to bother coming back to work if he wasn't going to do his share.
Lydia:	That sounds pretty drastic.
Matt:	I know. And I don't think it was fair since we weren't told what would be expected of us.
Lydia:	Are you sure you weren't told?
Matt:	I'm pretty sure I wasn't, but I don't know for sure about Simon. I suppose the fact that it was a charity golf outing should have warned us that something would be different about this event.
Lydia:	You know, the more you talk about this, the more it reminds me of one of Jesus' parables.
Matt:	Really? That seems like quite a stretch. I don't

	remember any parables about golf.
Lydia:	No, the parable wasn't about golf! It was about a wedding banquet.
Matt:	Which parable? And how does a story about a wedding reception remind you of my golf outing?
Lydia:	It's the parable from Matthew where a king throws a wedding banquet for his son. When it's time for the banquet, all the guests refuse to come for all kinds of bogus reasons. The king gets upset and invites a bunch of people off the streets to come to the banquet instead.
Matt:	So all of us management trainees are like these street people?
Lydia:	Right.
Matt:	Thanks for the compliment!
Lydia:	Not literally, Matt! Just for comparison purposes! And the comparison is that you all were invited to fill in for the top executives who didn't go. Then at the end of the parable, one of those people invited off the street is thrown out of the banquet because he didn't have on a wedding garment.
Matt:	That has never seemed fair to me. How was this person off the street supposed to have some fancy wedding clothes?
Lydia:	Maybe the king supplied the clothes, but this guest refused to put them on.
Matt:	Maybe. So you think my friend Simon is like this guest — he accepted the invitation, but refused to go along with what was expected of him?
Lydia:	Yes, doesn't that seem similar?

Matt: If you say so! I still don't think that either my golfing incident or that parable is fair. Isn't God's grace supposed to be a free gift? Why the insistence on wearing the wedding garment?

Lydia: I don't know about how your company treated you and Simon. I think they should have made clear what was expected of you. I agree that the parable doesn't sound fair either, but I think Matthew is trying to tell us that even if God's grace is free, God does expect us to respond to this free gift with faithfulness in return.

Matt: So God's grace prompts a grateful response from us?

Lydia: Yes. That's why Jesus says, "Many are called but few are chosen." The king invited many, but many of them refused the invitation. Only a few accepted the invitation and reacted with a grateful response.

Matt: So the question is: "Are we among the many or the few?" And "How have we responded to God's free gift of grace?"

Lydia: Yes, those are the questions: "Are we among the many or the few?" and "How have we responded to God's free gift of grace?"

Week 5

The Great Judgment

Matthew 25:31-46

Matt and Lydia are sitting down to dinner together after long days at work.

Lydia: How was your day?

Matt: Okay, I guess. Nothing special.

Lydia: Mine was special.

Matt: It was? How was it special?

Lydia: I saw Jesus!

Matt: Pardon me — what did you say?

Lydia: I said that I saw Jesus.

Matt: Are you serious?

Lydia: Yes!

Matt: Did you take some more of that cold medicine that makes you feel loopy?

Lydia: No.

Matt: I'll bet you were at church and were looking at that spot on the wall of the Fellowship Hall where the water has been seeping in and leaving a mark that looks like the face of a man.

Lydia: No.

Matt: I know. As part of your Lenten observance you went downtown to the Art Institute[1] and made a point of looking at the way Jesus has been portrayed in famous works of art. Who did you look

	at? Roualt, Rembrandt, or Raphael?
Lydia:	No, I didn't go downtown, although you have a good idea. Maybe I will go to the Art Institute before Lent is over. But I'll bet you saw Jesus today too.
Matt:	Okay, I'll humor you. When or where do you think I saw Jesus?
Lydia:	Let me ask you about your day first. Did you give that JCPenney's[2] gift certificate to your custodian?
Matt:	Yes, I did. He was very grateful — he said that they can really use it to get clothes for their new baby.
Lydia:	Good. I thought that would help them with their baby. Did you have your luncheon meeting with that group that's working with Amnesty International on writing letters to get prisoners of conscience released?
Matt:	Yes. It was a good meeting, and we got some letters written for one prisoner in Myanmar and another one in Zimbabwe.
Lydia:	Good. I hope it helps.
Matt:	I do too. You never know for sure, but they say that letters help at least improve their situation quite often.
Lydia:	Did you see your favorite person at the train station?
Matt:	Do you mean Elsie, the homeless person who's always playing on a recorder?
Lydia:	Yes.
Matt:	Yes, I did see her. I had an extra sandwich from

our luncheon meeting that no one touched, so I gave it to her.

Lydia: See, I told you that you saw Jesus.

Matt: Okay, Lydia, enough fooling around. What do you mean?

Lydia: It's all obvious if you stop to think about it. I got the idea on the way home tonight. I stopped to visit Irene's mother in the assisted living center I pass on the way home from work.

Matt: How is she?

Lydia: She's doing pretty well for someone who can get around only with a walker.

Matt: Did you have a good visit?

Lydia: We did. We always have interesting conversations. I love talking with her about her memories when she was growing up 75 years ago, and she loves English mysteries as much as I do.

Matt: But how did that lead to all this seeing Jesus stuff? Did she see Jesus when she was growing up?

Lydia: No, no, that's not it. When we were talking, she mentioned how lonely it is for most of the people in the home where she lives. She has a number of visitors, partly because Irene visits a lot, but she says that many of the people on her ward rarely have anyone come to see them.

Matt: That's so sad.

Lydia: It is, so I decided that I should stop more often and visit another resident besides Irene's mother each time I stop.

Matt: That sounds like a good idea. It wouldn't be out

	of your way.
Lydia:	Right, so I visited the woman in the next room for a while. And that's when I saw Jesus.
Matt:	What? You had a vision in the nursing home?
Lydia:	It's an "assisted living center." But no, I didn't have a vision exactly. What I had was a memory — a memory of one of Jesus' parables.
Matt:	Which one?
Lydia:	The one where the king judges the nations at the end of time like a shepherd separating the sheep from the goats.
Matt:	Isn't that the one where he tells the sheep that when he was hungry or thirsty they fed him, but they don't remember doing it?
Lydia:	Yes, and he condemns those on the goat side for not doing those things to him, but they can't remember ever not feeding him or not giving him clothes.
Matt:	I think the light is beginning to dawn. Didn't Jesus say then that whenever they fed or clothed "one of the least of these, his brothers and sisters," they had fed or clothed him?
Lydia:	Exactly. When I thought about the lonely people in the assisted living center, it struck me that they must be like "the least of these, my brothers and sisters," Jesus was talking about. So, if visiting them is visiting Jesus, then I saw Jesus today.
Matt:	And likewise, if clothing my custodian's baby, or feeding Elsie, or visiting the prisoners of conscience with a letter is like clothing or feeding or

visiting Jesus, then I saw Jesus today too. Actually, I saw him at least three times more than you did today.

Lydia: Right, but don't get a big head about it!

Matt: That suggests a question we can ask every morning.

Lydia: What's that?

Matt: Who are "the least of these" in whom I will encounter Jesus today?

Lydia: Yes, that's the question: Who are "the least of these" in whom I will encounter Jesus today?

---

1. The Art Institute of Chicago. Substitute the name of the nearest art museum or collection of religious paintings.

2. Substitute another familiar department store in your area.

From Discourse to Dialogue —

***Sermons from the
Five "Books" of Matthew***

Week 1

The Sermon on the Mount

Matthew 5:13-30

Narrator: Angela has been talking for months with her friend Matt about her church and her Christian faith. Matt has seemed vaguely interested but so far is unwilling to come to her church. He said that he thought he should read something about Jesus, and she suggested reading one of the gospels, starting with the first one, Matthew. That was a couple weeks ago, and she's been wondering how the reading project is going. She meets Matt as she's leaving the gym where they work out and he's coming in. Matt's carrying a camping lantern.

Angela: Hi, Matt! Why in the world are you bringing a lantern to the gym?

Matt: Hi, Angela. I could ask you the same question in reverse. Why aren't you carrying a lantern as you leave the gym?

Angela: That's easy. I'm not carrying a lantern because I'm not going camping in the woods, at least not in this weather. So why do you have a lantern?

Matt: It's all your fault. You wanted me to read one of the gospels, and I started with Matthew.

Angela: I still don't see why you have a lantern at the gym.

Matt: I'm just trying to do what Jesus said in the Sermon on the Mount.

Angela: I don't think he said, "Carry a lantern to the gym."

Matt: No, but he did say, "Let your light shine before others."

Angela: Oh, I get it. But Matt, that's a metaphor. Jesus didn't mean it literally. What does he go on to say? "...so that they may see your good works and give glory to your Father in heaven." It means that we're supposed to show our faith in our lives as if we were shining a light. We hope that people who see the light of our faith will come to believe too.

Matt: That's a relief. I was going to look pretty silly carrying this lantern around. I'll put it back in the car before I go in, but first I have a couple more questions.

Angela: Okay, I hope I can answer them.

Matt: I'm sure you probably can. I thought you told me that your church teaches that we're saved by faith, not by obeying a bunch of laws. But Jesus says that he came to fulfill the Law, not destroy it, and we can't be saved if our righteousness doesn't exceed the righteousness of the Pharisees. Who were they, by the way?

Angela: The Pharisees were a group of Jews in Jesus' day who were very pious and wanted to encourage Jews to keep all the laws in the Bible.

Matt: Okay, but why does Jesus say we have to keep the whole Law if we're saved by faith?

Angela: A good question.

Matt: I thought so.

Angela: Try this: Having faith means being in a trusting relationship with God. That trusting relationship is made possible by what Jesus did for us. When we live with this kind of trust, we want to live the way God wants us to. The Law shows us what God wants.

Matt: So if we have a loving, trusting relationship with God, we'll want to do what God wants, and keeping the whole Law is doing what God wants.

Angela: Right!

Matt: Okay, I get it, I guess. But I can't do it.

Angela: I can't either, but why do you say that?

Matt: You know what I think of my brother. He always annoys me, and I'm always calling him a jerk. So now Jesus says I'm as bad as a murderer.

Angela: Yes, Jesus' words are tough. A little later you'll read that Jesus says that we should love God with our whole heart. I think that's what Jesus means here. Obeying God isn't just following some checklist of what we're supposed to do or not do. Obeying God is having our heart in the right place and letting that affect everything we do.

Matt: So I can't call my brother a jerk any more?

Angela: Not to his face, anyway.

Matt: I don't know, Angela. I think Jesus is talking about our thoughts too. In the next section he says that someone who looks at a woman with lust in his heart is committing adultery. It seems to me that even calling my brother a jerk behind his back gets me in trouble with Jesus.

Angela: Maybe I shouldn't have told you to read Mat-

	thew! You are taking it seriously, aren't you?
Matt:	Isn't that what you wanted?
Angela:	Not if it gave *me* so much to think about! Well, back to that jerk — I mean, your dear brother. You might think about how you can love and respect your brother even if he annoys you.
Matt:	I suppose I can try to do that, even if he says or does things that upset me. But my thoughts — am I supposed to reform them too?
Angela:	Well, loving someone with your whole heart will affect how you think about them too, and thoughts can affect words and actions.
Matt:	These are tough words. Do you think Jesus really meant us to follow them perfectly?
Angela:	I do think Jesus meant what he said, but I also think he was describing an ideal for believers — an ideal that's beyond us but that we can strive for. And remember that God is totally gracious and forgiving. Do you always accomplish your workout goals?
Matt:	No, and when I do, my trainer always increases what I'm supposed to do.
Angela:	Does your trainer tell you not to come back if you don't do everything he wanted?
Matt:	No, he wants me to keep trying.
Angela:	God too. Because we have a loving relationship with God, Jesus wants us to keep trying to love God and others with our whole heart.
Matt:	Okay, but maybe I should put my lantern back in my car so that I can get to my workout.
Angela:	Yes, you should, but how do you think you can

	"let your light shine" during your workout?
Matt:	Maybe with an "attitude adjustment."
Angela:	What do you mean?
Matt:	It seems to me that loving God and others with our whole heart means having an attitude of love and respect toward others. So no more muttering under my breath and calling my trainer a jerk when he's just trying to help me improve. And no more hogging the equipment for myself and not sharing it with others. And maybe trying to help someone struggling with their workouts instead of making fun of them behind their backs.
Angela:	Wow! You have got lots of ways to shine light even without your lantern!
Matt:	And visiting the gym can be a physical workout and a faith workout too!
Angela:	I hope both workouts go well!

Week 2

Instructions for Disciples

Matthew 10:5-20

Narrator: Once again Angela meets her friend Matt after she's completed her workout and he's just coming to their gym. You'll recall that Angela suggested that Matt read the gospel of Matthew to learn more about Jesus.

Angela: Oh hi, Matt. It's good to see you again! What are you carrying with you this time? Is that a cow bell?

Matt: No, but you're close — it's a sheep bell.[1]

Angela: Where did you get a sheep bell?

Matt: A friend of mine brought it back from New Zealand as a souvenir.

Angela: That's cool, but my real question is, *why* are you carrying a sheep bell?

Matt: You should know — and I'm surprised you aren't carrying one.

Angela: Let me guess: Does this have something to do with your reading the gospel of Matthew?

Matt: You're very perceptive.

Angela: What have you been reading in Matthew now?

Matt: I'm reading the chapter where Jesus gives his disciples instructions for what to do to be his followers, and he says that he's sending them out to be like sheep among wolves. It seems only logical that I should be carrying a sheep bell if I want

	to follow Jesus — and be like a sheep among wolves.
Angela:	You seem to need a lesson on metaphors! Jesus sends his disciples out *like* sheep among wolves, not as actual sheep.
Matt:	Okay, what does Jesus mean then?
Angela:	I have to admit that the image is not all that encouraging. Jesus is warning his disciples that the world may be hostile to them. Just as sheep have predators, followers of Jesus may have people who oppose or dislike them.
Matt:	And you want me to be a follower of Christ?
Angela:	Yes! I believe that the benefits of following Christ far outweigh the risks.
Matt:	Okay, if you say so. But let me ask you something. Why are you using that backpack?
Angela:	To carry my workout clothes. Why do you ask?
Matt:	Jesus told his disciples not to use bags for their journey. Are you going to tell me that was a metaphor too?
Angela:	Yes and no.
Matt:	What kind of an answer is that? Either it is a metaphor or it isn't.
Angela:	I think it wasn't a metaphor just then for the first disciples. He wanted them to rely on the hospitality of the people with whom they shared the message about Jesus. It was a way for them to see how receptive the people were to their message. Another time Jesus told the disciples to be sure to take a bag and other necessities on their

	mission trips. No, it wasn't a metaphor in that sense.
Matt:	But it was a metaphor in another sense?
Angela:	Yes. I think Jesus wants us to travel "light" — not to be weighed down with all sorts of things we think that we have to do or say.
Matt:	But don't disciples need to do or say something? We're not like statues!
Angela:	That's right. We're supposed to be ready to say or do what is necessary to express God's love in whatever situation we find ourselves.
Matt:	How in the world can we know what that might be?
Angela:	We don't have to know.
Matt:	We don't?
Angela:	No. Doesn't Jesus tell them that God's Spirit will speak through them?
Matt:	Yes, he does.
Angela:	So, don't worry about having all the right things to say. Be ready for God's Spirit to give you the words to say — or the actions to perform.
Matt:	But how do I know that the words that come to me are from God's Spirit rather than some evil spirit?
Angela:	Good question!
Matt:	Sheep bell or not, I want my words to ring true.
Angela:	Your words will ring true if they follow what God wants.
Matt:	What might that be?

Angela: That may change from time to time, but doesn't Jesus tell the disciples to heal people and bring them peace?

Matt: Yes, he does.

Angela: Then the Spirit will give us words to say or actions to perform that bring people God's healing or peace.

Matt: But Jesus says later that he came not to bring peace but a sword.

Angela: That seems contradictory, doesn't it?

Matt: Yes, it does!

Angela: Remember being a sheep in a hostile world. Not everyone appreciates God's message of love and peace for all people, and they react negatively.

Matt: Peace that's not peaceful? Do we really want that?

Angela: Yes, because the joy of following Jesus is worth far more than any difficulty it might bring.

Matt: Just like the satisfaction of having a good workout goes beyond whatever pain it causes.

Angela: Right! Work until it hurts.

Matt: So being a sheep among wolves might mean trying to bring peace between people who are at each other's throats — like some of the people in my workout group.

Angela: Yes, it might.

Matt: Or some of the talk in the locker room can be pretty nasty about people they don't like. Maybe being a sheep among wolves means suggesting some way to heal what causes that nastiness.

Angela: Another good — but not easy — idea. I'll let you go to your workout now, but you can put your bell away!

Matt: Maybe I'll keep the bell in case I need it to ring for help to escape the wolves in the locker room!

---

1. If a sheep bell is not available, find another kind of bell and adjust the text accordingly.

Week 3

Parables of the Kingdom

Matthew 13:10-17, 31-33

Narrator: Today we find Matt in a local grocery store picking something up for dinner when he runs into Angela in the aisle with baking supplies.

Matt: Hi, Angela! I didn't expect to see you here.

Angela: Oh hi, Matt! I didn't expect to see you either.

Matt: What are you shopping for?

Angela: I'm looking for some yeast. I'm baking the bread for Communion next Sunday.

Matt: Can you use regular baked bread for Communion?

Angela: Sure. We usually use unleavened bread, but leavened bread is okay too.

Matt: That reminds me. I was reading some more in Matthew.

Angela: And that has something to do with yeast?

Matt: Sure. Don't you remember Jesus' parable about how the kingdom of heaven is like a woman putting leaven in her bread?

Angela: Oh, right. It's not one of the most famous parables.

Matt: It isn't? At least it's short. But that doesn't make it easier to understand.

Angela: No, I suppose not.

Matt: In fact, I don't understand why Jesus taught in

parables at all.

Angela: I always thought it was because he wanted to use everyday, ordinary examples to make his message easier to understand.

Matt: Is that what you think? Apparently you haven't read Matthew recently!

Angela: You've got me there! Why do you say that?

Matt: Because if you read the chapter in Matthew where Jesus teaches in a bunch of parables, he says that he uses parables precisely so that people *don't* understand him.

Angela: Really? I had forgotten that.

Matt: You know, I think Jesus could use a better marketing person.

Angela: Why do you think so?

Matt: Didn't you tell me to read Matthew so that I could know more about Jesus?

Angela: Yes.

Matt: And don't you want me to know more about Jesus so that maybe I might worship more at your church and maybe even become a member?

Angela: Well, yes, but only if you agree to it; I'm not trying to force you into something.

Matt: I appreciate that, but it seems from Matthew that Jesus isn't all that interested in promoting his message. It's like he's keeping it secret except for a few select followers.

Angela: This reminds me of *Harry Potter* or *The Lord of the Rings*.

Matt: It does?

Angela: Remember how you said that you couldn't get into those books or movies because you don't like fantasy like that?

Matt: That's right. Now take *Star Trek*. That makes more sense to me.

Angela: And it turns me off. But that's my point.

Matt: What's your point?

Angela: During his ministry, Jesus often faced opposition. People didn't like what he preached or were upset when he went against religious customs of his day. So he preached in parables so that people who opposed him or who weren't really interested in hearing his message wouldn't get it, but people who wanted to understand him might be puzzled by the parable but would be open to learning what he meant.

Matt: So his parables weren't meant for everyone, only for those who wanted to listen to him.

Angela: Right.

Matt: How does that explain the parable about the mustard seed or the leaven in the bread?

Angela: I don't know if your marketing person would approve or not. A mustard seed is not the most glitzy image, but it is about growth.

Matt: Right — growth into a big bush!

Angela: But it symbolizes something the Bible says over and over again.

Matt: What's that?

Angela: God often takes something or someone small and insignificant — like a mustard seed — and uses it to do something really important — like the seed

	becoming a large bush and sheltering a bunch of birds.
Matt:	So God could use me to do something really important?
Angela:	That's right.
Matt:	Wait a minute — are you saying that I'm small and insignificant?
Angela:	You said it, not me! Whether that's true of you or not, God did similar things with Jesus and the twelve disciples and Mary and lots of others in the Bible.
Matt:	"Lots of others in the Bible" — are you trying to get me to read more of the Bible?
Angela:	That's not a bad idea, but you can stick with Matthew for now. When you do read more of the Bible, you'll see how God works through flawed and imperfect people — like Jacob who tricked his brother out of his inheritance, or Moses who didn't like public speaking, or King David who started out as a shepherd boy — or prophets like Amos who was a farmer and Jeremiah who was a boy when he began to prophesy. Then there are Jesus' disciples who were fishermen and Matthew, one of the tax collectors who most people hated. So there's hope for important things from you and me too!
Matt:	That's hopeful, I guess, even if it's not exactly complimentary. But what do you mean by including Jesus in your list? He's the Son of God, isn't he?
Angela:	Yes, but he was born in a stable and grew up in a poor family in a backwater town in Galilee.

Matt: So what about the yeast?

Angela: That's something apparently insignificant too, yet it spreads through all the dough and makes the bread rise. Our faith may seem insignificant, but it can spread throughout us to transform us, and it can spread throughout a congregation or community and change it too. God can use little things to accomplish big tasks.

Matt: So I can expect my faith to transform me and change the world?

Angela: That sounds a little more ambitious than I meant, but I agree. You have to watch out for what God will do with you!

Matt: Well, I hope that yeast works in your bread dough. I'll look forward to seeing your bread next Sunday.

Angela: And I look forward to seeing what great things God will do even through you!

Matt: And even through you too!

Week 4

Instructions for the Church

Matthew 18:1-14

Narrator: Last Saturday the scouts were having a pancake breakfast in town, and Angela ran into Matt, who was there helping with his nephew's Cub Scout pack.

Angel: Hi, Matt! I didn't know you had anything to do with the scouts.

Matt: Hi, Angela! Thanks for coming! Yes, I've been helping with the Cub Scout pack for about two years now, ever since my nephew joined.

Angela: Well, scouting is a great program. I still remember the things I learned as a Girl Scout.

Matt: I think Matthew would agree with you.

Angela: What do you mean? I don't recall a reference to scouts in Matthew.

Matt: No, Matthew doesn't mention scouts. But Jesus does say, "Unless you change and become like children, you will never enter the kingdom of heaven." Do you think Jesus would want me always to wear my scout uniform?

Angela: You in a scout uniform? That's a scary thought! Besides, I don't think they had scouts or uniforms back then.

Matt: I suppose not. What do you think it means? Some people think children are innocent. I don't think that I can pretend to be innocent.

Angela: It wouldn't hurt for you to behave so that you might seem innocent, but the Bible doesn't usually talk about anyone, even children, as being innocent. Being sinful pretty much applies to everyone.

Matt: That's true enough. I love kids and I enjoy working with scouts, but by this age at least they aren't all that innocent. Is that what Jesus means — that we should be as wild and unruly as a bunch of scouts left by themselves?

Angela: No, I don't think Jesus means that either. Are your scouts that bad?

Matt: Not really. They can also be spontaneous and creative and energetic. "Innocent" just doesn't describe them. If not innocent, what are we to be then?

Angela: I've always thought Jesus meant that we should be trusting. Just as children need to depend on their parents and trust them to take care of them, so we are to trust and depend on God.

Matt: That makes sense. I noticed that Jesus talks about being "humble" like a child. Why would he emphasize humility? I don't know that all my scouts are humble. Some of the older ones can be mean to the younger ones.

Angela: That's helpful that you noticed that, Matt. What I said about being trusting isn't all that different from being humble. I think that Jesus isn't talking about someone *feeling* humble; I'll bet that he is referring to the humble *status* of children. We tend to pay a lot of attention to children today, but back in biblical times children weren't given much attention. Sometimes they were thought of as little more than property.

Matt: Let me tell you sometime about how I've seen children being treated now. I think we could give our children more healthy attention even today. But why should believers be of humble status? I'm not sure I want to be a believer if I'll have no status.

Angela: Jesus doesn't mean that we're not important. No, we're very important to God. It goes back to what I said about trust. Jesus often warns against believers thinking that they're better than others. The point is that all of us depend on God for life and forgiveness, and that our basic attitude as believers is an attitude of trust.

Matt: So just as children are humble because they are vulnerable and need to depend on others, we are to be humble by recognizing that we need to trust God.

Angela: Right. Notice too how Jesus favors children. If we feel unimportant or unworthy of God's love, Jesus assures us that God wants to embrace us and doesn't see us as unimportant or unworthy.

Matt: I wonder if this explains something else in the chapter I just read. Jesus tells another parable — this one about a shepherd with a hundred sheep. You said that parables are "earthly stories with a heavenly meaning." Well, if this parable is an earthly story, that shepherd is not too smart.

Angela: What do you mean?

Matt: Well, the shepherd has 100 sheep. One wanders away and he leaves the 99 alone while he goes off to find the one lost sheep. That's not very wise. What if some predator comes and kills off a bunch of the other sheep, or another shepherd steals most of them? Saving one lamb but losing a bunch of others doesn't sound wise to me.

Angela: Parables may be earthly stories, but they may be different enough from our ordinary experience to make us wonder what the point is.

Matt: I guess that's what I was thinking. Does this parable mean that God would go to great lengths to save someone who might seem unimportant to everyone else — someone of as humble status as children back then?

Angela: I think you've got it!

Matt: So if we're ever inclined to have doubts about whether or not we're important enough for God to care about us, this parable assures us that God does care.

Angela: Come to think about it, it's too bad there weren't scouts in Jesus' day.

Matt: Why do you say that? So that Jesus and the disciples could have had pancake breakfasts?

Angela: No! Especially not if there would be pork sausages!

Matt: Right, that would have been a problem.

Angela: What I mean is that scouts are children who learn to trust their leaders and their fellow scouts. They know they need to depend on each other. That's important for all of us — to recognize our need for God and to rely on one another for support and help. Being independent and self-sufficient

	is good, but many times going it alone can lead to arrogance or just plain trouble.
Matt:	You're right. Especially when we go camping, we teach our scouts to work together and rely on each other, but we also hope they learn skills that will help them take care of themselves.
Angela:	Sure, but some of those skills are for the sake of watching out for each other. So if someone is having a problem, other scouts are there to help out. That's important for all of us too — to keep an eye out for someone who needs a helping hand.
Matt:	So we could rewrite Matthew and have Jesus say, "Be good scouts"?
Angela:	I don't think I'd go that far, but it's not a bad idea. But speaking about children and sheep, there's a bunch of scouts over there just sitting around not doing anything.
Matt:	You're right. I'd better get back on the job and assign them some work to do. Did you get enough pancakes? And don't forget our raffle as you leave!

Week 5

Warnings of Final Judgment

Matthew 24:1-35

Narrator: It's a Friday night and Angela and Matt happen to meet each other again, this time at the VFW Friday night fish fry.

Matt: Oh hi, Angela! It's good to see you again.

Angela: Well hi, Matt! We seem to keep running into each other.

Matt: First the grocery store, then the pancake breakfast, and now this.

Angela: There seems to be a food theme here.

Matt: No wonder we also spend a lot of time at the gym!

Angela: Do you often come to the VFW fish fry?

Matt: Yes, I do. For some reason Fridays and fish fries go together for me.

Angela: For me too. Do you belong to the VFW?

Matt: No, but my grandfather did — he was a World War II veteran — so I like to support the VFW. What about you?

Angela: Personally I'm not connected, but I have friends from church who are members and I have family members who are veterans.

Matt: I thought maybe you were here because of Matthew.

Angela: Because of Matthew? I know they caught fish in

	biblical times, and I suppose they ate them, but I don't recall any fish fries.
Matt:	I'm not talking about frying fish; I'm talking about the part where Jesus mentions "wars and rumors of wars."
Angela:	Oh, you're reading *that* chapter.
Matt:	Yes, I've just read the chapter where Jesus talks about the end of the world. There's some scary stuff there. I thought you said your church doesn't do "hellfire and brimstone."
Angela:	We don't really, and I don't think Matthew does exactly either, although that sermon of Jesus does talk about the end of time.
Matt:	And eating here in the VFW hall does remind me that we have known lots of "wars and rumors of wars." So does your church encourage people to sit around and wait for the end of the world?
Angela:	No, it doesn't, and neither does Jesus. People in Jesus' day were expecting the world to end soon. If I remember correctly, Jesus warned his disciples against people who predicted that the world was ending soon. He told them that other things had to happen first.
Matt:	Yes, he said that the good news about God's kingdom had to be preached throughout the world first. But he did talk about signs of the end — wars, catastrophes, persecution. Lots of grim stuff. And then something about a fig tree and summer.
Angela:	Oh, right. Maybe it's not easy thinking of summer when it's still so wintry out, but when trees start sprouting leaves you know that summer is

not far away. Yes, Jesus says that we should pay attention to signs of the end and be ready, but not to get too excited. When the end comes is up to God.

Matt: So if the people at your church aren't sitting around waiting for the end to come, what's the point of Jesus' sermon?

Angela: Well, remember what I said about Jesus discouraging too much anxiousness about the end of the world. One point is not to worry about the end because it will happen according to God's good time.

Matt: Yes, but Jesus still talks about the end.

Angela: Right. We do believe that Jesus will return at the end of time, and another point of Jesus' sermon is that we should be ready — yes, ready for the end of the world, but also ready for our own end. Life is fragile and sitting here in the VFW hall surely can remind us of that. Anyone who has been in war knows the terror and the danger of combat.

Matt: That's true enough, and nowadays there's too much shooting on our streets and in our schools and even stores.

Angela: Yes, but in spite of that Jesus tells us that we can trust in God. Doesn't he say something about "heaven and earth will pass away, but my words will not pass away"? In other words, we can trust Jesus' and God's promises because they are forever and will last beyond the whole world.

Matt: Jesus does say that, but he also says that his generation will not pass away before all these things

	happen. If that's true, why is the world still here?
Angela:	That's a difficult verse, isn't it?
Matt:	I thought so.
Angela:	The explanation that makes sense to me is that the world did end.
Matt:	What? I don't think so — unless you're saying this fish fry is in heaven.
Angela:	No, I'm not saying that. What I mean is that when Jesus rose from the dead, it was a signal that the old world was defeated and the new world of life in Christ had begun.
Matt:	So the resurrection of Jesus marked the end of the old world and the beginning of the new?
Angela:	Right, although it's more accurate to say that believers live in two worlds now. The old world continues, but Jesus' resurrection ushered in the new world he promised.
Matt:	So we don't have to worry about the end because we already know how it's going to turn out?
Angela:	Yes, but that doesn't mean the path through the end will be easy; it does mean that we can count on God to go with us and to keep God's promises.
Matt:	How are we supposed to be ready for the end, then?
Angela:	One way is to hold on to God's promise to be with us, whether it's our end or the world's end.
Matt:	Okay, and there's another way?
Angela:	Yes, another way is to live like the world has already ended.

Matt: You don't mean that we should act like ghosts or something, do you?

Angela: You sound like my little nephew who's all obsessed with zombies! No, I don't mean that. I mean that we should live a life full of the love and forgiveness that Jesus began with his resurrection.

Matt: Are you suggesting that a way to be ready for the end is to come to your church and celebrate Easter?

Angela: Well, that is one way! Since we seem to meet around food, will I see you next at our Easter breakfast?

*Mysteries of Matthew:
Proclaiming "Both" to the
Gospel's Balancing Act*

Mysteries of Matthew: Proclaiming "Both" to the Gospel's Balancing Act was inspired by noticing how often Matthew seems to want to balance the newness of Jesus' message with its reinforcing of Old Testament faith and practice. Each dialogue in this series takes up a different aspect of Matthew's "balancing act," and the characters advocate for each competing emphasis with a final "proclamation" that Matthew intends to affirm both emphases.

Matt and Eunice are reading through the gospel of Matthew as part of their Lenten devotions, since this year is the "Year of Matthew." The gospel of Matthew often seems to be balancing competing emphases; "Matt" and "Eunice" ("Matt" + "hew") represent those differing tendencies.

Week 1

Turning Cheeks or Resisting Evil?

Matthew 5:38-48

Narrator: Matt and Eunice have just finished reading tonight's lesson from Jesus' Sermon on the Mount. The gospel of Matthew often seems to be balancing competing emphases; "Matt" and "Eunice" ("Matt" + "hew") represent those differing tendencies.

Eunice: Do you think Jesus really expects us to live like this?

Matt: Live like what?

Eunice: Like loving enemies.

Matt: Well, yes. Why would he preach this sermon if he didn't expect us to follow what he says?

Eunice: His Sermon on the Mount surely isn't easy to follow.

Matt: It is difficult, but that doesn't mean that we shouldn't try.

Eunice: Loving enemies seems so contrary to human nature. How can I have caring thoughts and feelings toward someone who has hurt me?

Matt: Christian love may be contrary to human nature, but remember that when Jesus says "love your neighbor" or "love your enemy," he's not saying that you should want to hug them.

Eunice: So if someone bullies me or purposely insults me, I don't have to go and hug them?

Matt: No, Jesus doesn't mean love like that.

Eunice: That's a relief! But what *does* he mean?

Matt: Christian love means an attitude toward others that seeks what's best for them whether they deserve it or not. You might not *like* someone, but you can treat them with respect for your common humanity. Or better yet, you can respect others as someone God created and someone for whom Jesus died and rose again, even if you don't particularly enjoy their company.

Eunice: Well, maybe I can learn to love my enemies in that way, but I don't think I can learn to "turn my other cheek" to someone who is abusing me.

Matt: What's the difference?

Eunice: Loving enemies is one thing, but "turning the other cheek" seems to imply that we should accept abusive treatment. I don't think that's right, and I can't imagine Jesus telling us that we should let others abuse us or bully us.

Matt: I don't think Jesus is talking about accepting abuse. He's trying to move beyond cycles of revenge. The Old Testament principle of "an eye for an eye" was trying to prevent the escalation of vengeance between people who were harming each other. Jesus was going a step further and urging us not to seek revenge.

Eunice: Telling us to "turn the other cheek" sounds like more than just not seeking revenge.

Matt: It would help if we knew more about what life was like in Jesus' time. I've heard it explained that if someone hit you on your right cheek, that would mean hitting you with the back of their hand — a way someone would hit a slave or someone inferior to them. "Turning your cheek" would invite them to hit you with their palm — a way you might fight with someone who is an equal. "Turning the other cheek" in that case means insisting on being treated with respect without seeking revenge.

Eunice: I see your point, although I would still be getting hit twice.

Matt: But the second time with respect!

Eunice: How wonderful! But how about giving away our clothes and going the second mile?

Matt: Roman soldiers had the right to demand that people give them their coats or carry backpacks a mile for them. Doing more was a way of asserting one's value as a person in the face of the soldier's attempt to abuse or belittle them.

Eunice: An interesting explanation, I suppose, but those soldiers would be getting away with more clothes and more free labor. Asserting my value this way would get me sore muscles and a naked body. It still seems to me that Jesus is encouraging us to let people get away with abuse.

Matt: I don't think so. I think Jesus is telling us not to resist evil violently — not to resist evil in the same way as the evildoer, but to overcome evil with good instead.

Eunice: So how am I supposed to deal with someone who bullies or belittles me? "Turning my other cheek" wouldn't mean much today.

Matt: No, it wouldn't, but first you could remember to "love your enemy" — that is, to remember as awful as they are, they are a person created and loved by God.

Eunice: Okay, so I won't demonize them.

Matt: Then "turning your other cheek" today means finding a way to stand up for yourself without returning the same kind of abuse.

Eunice: I think that's easy to say, but what would you tell my child who's being bullied in school?

Matt: Or a spouse who's being abused, or employees whose boss regularly humiliates them.

Eunice: Right! What would Jesus say to all them about cheek-turning?

Matt: I don't think there are easy answers, or some method that will help with every situation. But I think people can find some way to say, "I won't go along with your putting me down like this anymore. I expect you to treat me with respect, and I plan to treat you the same way." If the situation is dangerous or difficult, they may need help from other people.

Eunice: Do you think, then, that we can overcome evil without violence?

Matt: April 4th was not long ago. Do you remember what happened about fifty years ago on that day?

Eunice: Yes, Martin Luther King Jr. was assassinated.

Matt: Well, he believed in overcoming evil without violence.

Eunice: Right, and see what happened to him!

Matt: Yes, he was assassinated, but his nonviolent approach to the civil rights movement eventually led to important steps forward for civil rights for black Americans. Jesus is encouraging resistance to evil with love and without violence.

Eunice: So "turning the other cheek" doesn't have to mean giving in to abuse or bullying?

Matt: No! Resist evil, but without replying in kind.

Eunice: So should we resist evil?

Matt: Or should we "turn the other cheek"?

Both: Matthew says, "Both!"

Week 2

Don't Worry — Be Faithful

Matthew 6:24-34

Narrator: Matt and Eunice have just finished reading tonight's lesson from Jesus' Sermon on the Mount. The gospel of Matthew often seems to be balancing competing emphases; "Matt" and "Eunice" ("Matt" + "hew") represent those differing tendencies.

Eunice: Matt, I've been thinking about college.

Matt: You have? Do you want to get another bachelor's degree or are you thinking of graduate school?

Eunice: Not for me! For our grandchildren! Don't you think it would be wise to be setting up a savings account to put aside money for their college education? A college education is only going to get more expensive. I don't like to think of our grandchildren being saddled with huge student loan debt.

Matt: You worry too much! When the time comes, I'm sure our kids will find a way to finance their children's college education.

Eunice: How can you be sure? Our kids aren't good at saving money. Besides, we're at a point in life when we could set more money aside.

Matt: I still say you worry too much. Don't you remember that passage we just read from Matthew, "Don't worry about your life, what you will eat or what you will drink or what you will wear"?

Eunice: It didn't say anything about the costs of a college education.

Matt: Of course not. But if Jesus said not to worry about such basic costs as food and clothing, surely he would say that even more about extra expenses like college tuition.

Eunice: In our day and age I don't think college expenses are extra. Besides, I've always found this passage too unrealistic. How can we not worry about food and clothing?

Matt: Maybe *you* can't stop such worrying, but that doesn't mean Jesus isn't right! Jesus expects us to trust God to take care of us.

Eunice: Do you have life insurance?

Matt: You know that I do — we both do. What does that have to do with this passage?

Eunice: Doesn't that show that you're not trusting God to take care of us?

Matt: You've got a point. Generations ago people thought having life insurance conflicted with Christian faith. I don't think, though, that being wise about how we handle our financial planning, including having life insurance, means we don't trust God. We trust that God gave us good sense and expects us to use it. I still say, "Trust God — don't worry!"

Eunice: Do you remember the story of Jesus' temptation?

Matt: Yes, we just read that a couple chapters ago. What's that got to do with this passage? Are you trying to change the subject?

Eunice: No, I'm not changing the subject. I think you're doing something that Jesus refused to do because he saw it as a temptation.

Matt: What in the world do you mean? I'm suggesting that we trust God to take care of us and not be consumed with worry. Where's the devil in that?

Eunice: Remember how Jesus refused to throw himself off the pinnacle of the temple, even though the devil quoted God's promise that angels would save him? Jesus said, "You shall not tempt the Lord your God." If you refuse to worry about the future and make wise plans, aren't you tempting God to take care of things you should have taken care of?

Matt: There's quite a difference between risky behavior like jumping off a roof and refusing to be consumed with worry. I don't see how not worrying is tempting God.

Eunice: I can't believe, though, that Jesus doesn't expect us to use our good sense and make plans for how we're going to take care of ourselves and our families.

Matt: Maybe there's a difference between "worrying" and "making plans." You can make plans for the future without being anxious about what will happen.

Eunice: Maybe *you* can. I'm not sure I can.

Matt: Oh, you of little faith!

Eunice: That's not fair! I do believe, but I also believe in being prudent.

Matt: I know you believe. I think, though, that we both may be missing something here. It does have something to do with faith, or what we believe in.

Eunice: What do you mean?

Matt: Jesus begins this passage by saying you can't serve both God and wealth.

Eunice: And he concludes by telling us to "seek first God's kingdom and God's righteousness."

Matt: How we worry has something to do with what we put our trust in. If we're all consumed with accumulating wealth and possessions, then we might very well be anxious about keeping or increasing our wealth.

Eunice: But if we're seeking God and God's will, we might not be so consumed with what possessions we have.

Matt: We might not think that we worship other gods these days, but what we focus on with our worries might be something that functions like a god for us.

Eunice: Like your golf game, for example.

Matt: What are you talking about?

Eunice: Well, you worry a lot about how your golf is going, and you even "worship" on the golf course some Sunday mornings.

Matt: Whoa! I confess to focusing on golf sometimes, but I don't think it rises to divine status! And besides, I don't golf on Sundays very often.

Eunice: Okay, I'll give you a pass on your golf obsession, but I can see that accumulating wealth or status or popularity can so consume people's energy that they think of nothing else.

Matt: And then they worry about losing it or not having enough.

Eunice: We're not talking about reasonable planning but having our lives focused in the wrong place.

Matt: So Jesus is encouraging us to trust in God and not wealth or other false gods.

Eunice: And he's not saying that we shouldn't plan ahead — just be sure that our planning is not a sign of being committed to another god.

Matt: So should we not worry?

Eunice: Or should we make plans but have faith in God?

Both: Matthew says, "Both!"

Week 3

Only the Lost Sheep of the House of Israel?

Matthew 15:21-28

Narrator: Matt and Eunice have just finished reading tonight's lesson about the Canaanite woman. The gospel of Matthew often seems to be balancing competing emphases; "Matt" and "Eunice" ("Matt" + "hew") represent those differing tendencies.

Eunice: I don't understand this story.

Matt: What don't you understand? It seems pretty clear to me. A woman has a sick daughter and Jesus heals her.

Eunice: But why did Jesus refuse at first? That doesn't seem like Jesus, and his response seems a little rude.

Matt: I suppose it might seem that way. But Jesus couldn't help everyone.

Eunice: He couldn't? Why not?

Matt: Let me rephrase that; notice how even this Gentile woman calls him "Son of David." That title for Jesus suggests that his primary role was to bring God's message to his own people.

Eunice: Perhaps, but he often had conflicts with some of the religious leaders of his people.

Matt: That's why he said "the *lost sheep* of the house of Israel." Jesus wanted to call them back to following God faithfully. Remember how he said in the Sermon on the Mount that he did not come to abolish the Law but to fulfill it. You know, Jesus is similar to prophets like Isaiah and Jeremiah — he wanted his people to love God with their whole heart.

Eunice: Well, if that's the whole point of Matthew's gospel, why does it begin with Gentile magi from the East coming to worship him right after he was born?

Matt: Hmmm, that is an interesting point. But remember that they came to worship "the King of the Jews."

Eunice: Do you think, then, that Jesus was wrong to give in to this Gentile woman and heal her daughter? Was he wrong to take some of the children's bread and let it fall to the ground as crumbs for the little dogs?

Matt: No, I don't think he was wrong to heal her daughter. After all, it was in his nature to show compassion. Comparing the Gentiles to dogs was a little harsh, but Jesus often used picturesque and exaggerated language. And I think he was expressing his view of his primary mission — primary, but not exclusive. You're a sales rep for your company. What area do you cover?

Eunice: I cover the Chicago metropolitan area from Kenosha County in Wisconsin to Lake County in Indiana. What's that got to do with Matthew?

Matt: Well, if I asked you to sell something to my sister in Kalamazoo, Michigan, would you do it?

Eunice: I don't know — is her credit better than yours?

Matt: My credit's not that bad! But yes, her credit is

	better than mine.
Eunice:	That's good! Then I might sell it to you to give to your sister, but I'd probably refer you to the person who handles sales in Michigan.
Matt:	Right. So you're not opposed to people in Michigan buying your product; it's just someone else's responsibility. Jesus is saying his primary purpose is to call "the lost sheep of the house of Israel" back to God. Later it will be his disciples' responsibility to reach out to Gentiles too.
Eunice:	That reminds me of the end of Matthew's gospel that I had to memorize in Confirmation class: "Go therefore and make disciples of all nations, baptizing them in the name of the Father, and the Son, and the Holy Spirit, teaching them to obey everything I have commanded you."
Matt:	Exactly. So Jesus begins with his base. Matthew keeps on showing us how what he says and does connects with the Old Testament, but that doesn't keep his message from being shared with all Gentiles.
Eunice:	And Matthew shows this reaching out to all people by beginning with the Gentile wise men and finishing with Jesus' sending his disciples to all nations.
Matt:	So what should we do? Like Jesus, serving the "lost sheep of the house of Israel," and like you, supplying the needs of clients in your service area, I think we should also "serve our base." Right here in our own congregation we have lots of needs — I know several people who are unemployed, and we have people who are homebound or in the hospital.

Eunice: We could make quite a list — people who are grieving, people dealing with family problems, people who could use some help in sharing their faith with their children.

Matt: "Serving our base" can refer to our community too. If we don't think there are enough needs for us to work on in our congregation, we can find plenty to do in our town.

Eunice: I can't deny that there are a lot of opportunities for us to show God's love in our own congregation and town, but I think we're missing the point of Matthew if that's the extent of our focus.

Matt: How are we missing the point if we are sharing God's love?

Eunice: Because God's love doesn't have limits or boundaries. God's love keeps pushing us beyond our comfort zone. God's love shines a light on the needs of people whether they are different from us or distant from us.

Matt: You know, I only have so much time or energy.

Eunice: That sounds like an excuse to be lazy!

Matt: That's not fair! It seems reasonable for me to focus on the needs of people in my immediate church or community.

Eunice: Of course, we can't do everything, but that doesn't mean we should shut our eyes to how people need help beyond our "service area."

Matt: You sound unrealistic to me!

Eunice: That's not fair either! There are lots of examples of Christians reaching out to help people far beyond their "service area" — like the campaigns to fight malaria and HIV/AIDS in Africa.

Matt: What should we do then? Serve our base...

Eunice: Or reach out to others beyond our own community?

Both: Matthew says, "Both!"

Week 4

How Often Should We Forgive?

Matthew 18:15-35

Narrator: Matt and Eunice have just finished reading tonight's lesson about forgiveness. The gospel of Matthew often seems to be balancing competing emphases; "Matt" and "Eunice" ("Matt" + "hew") represent those differing tendencies.

Matt: I told you, you should forgive me.

Eunice: What are you talking about?

Matt: Didn't you hear what Jesus told Peter?

Eunice: Yes, he told Peter to forgive seventy times seven. You think that applies to us?

Matt: Of course I do. Aren't we supposed to apply the Bible to our lives?

Eunice: Yes, we are, but do you think this applies to all those ways you continually annoy me?

Matt: Jesus doesn't seem to distinguish between kinds of sins; he just says to forgive an impossible number of times.

Eunice: But you don't change and you never say you're sorry.

Matt: Jesus doesn't say not to forgive if the other person doesn't say they're sorry.

Eunice: Oh, yes, he does! Remember how he said that if someone sins against you, you should talk with them alone and see if they will repent. If they don't, then talk with them with a couple others,

	and then with the whole church. If they don't repent of how they've hurt you, then they can be thrown out of the church. That doesn't sound like forgiving without repentance!
Matt:	Are you trying to get me excommunicated because I annoy you sometimes?
Eunice:	Hmm, there's an idea. No, I don't want you to be kicked out of the church because you're so annoying, but this forgiveness business is more complicated than you say.
Matt:	That's probably true. But confronting someone about how they've hurt you is not the same as not forgiving them.
Eunice:	It's not?
Matt:	No, it's not. You can forgive someone and still try to deal with whatever hurt or upset you.
Eunice:	I thought the motto was "Forgive and forget."
Matt:	If someone really hurt you, it's unlikely that you'll forget it. You can forgive but not forget.
Eunice:	I suppose the "forget" in the proverb means not to obsess over something or cling to some hurt forever.
Matt:	Right, and sometimes when people have been hurt, they'll say, "It doesn't matter." But if it's something serious, it does matter.
Eunice:	Then you're supposed to forgive too?
Matt:	Yes...
Eunice:	But you're supposed to talk with the person to encourage their repentance.
Matt:	Yes, but still forgive. Remember Pope John Paul II.

Eunice: What about him?

Matt: Do you remember when he visited Mehmet Ali Agca, the man who tried to assassinate him?

Eunice: Yes, I remember the picture of them sitting face-to-face.

Matt: Well, the pope forgave him — but he didn't say it didn't matter, and he didn't say he'd forget it, and he didn't try to get him out of prison.

Eunice: What is forgiveness, then, if it's none of those things?

Matt: Forgiveness is letting go of your anger over what happened to you and leaving any consequences up to God.

Eunice: I don't think you go far enough.

Matt: You don't? Why not?

Eunice: Remember how Jesus says you should confront the person who sinned against you so that you regain that person as a brother or sister. Just releasing your anger up to God won't accomplish that.

Matt: No, it won't, but it's not always possible to accomplish that. What if the person we need to forgive lives in another state or has died or doesn't feel sorry for what they did? We still need to forgive them.

Eunice: I suppose we do but is that really full forgiveness? I think full forgiveness means confronting someone and working out the differences between us.

Matt: I agree that's the ideal, but I don't think it's always realistic.

Eunice: How about us? Is it so unrealistic for you to work on being less annoying?

Matt: Wait a minute! Do I really annoy you that much, or do I just have quirky but endearing characteristics?

Eunice: Let me explain to you the difference between your endearing and annoying characteristics —

Matt: Is this the time to go into this? Besides, you're no perfect person either!

Eunice: So I annoy you too?

Matt: Sometimes!

Eunice: Why don't we plan a time when we can talk this out? Then our forgiving each other can be more complete.

Matt: That sounds good to me, but I still say that we are supposed to forgive even if we can't work out what bothers us.

Eunice: That's a cop-out!

Matt: Not always. I still remember a kid in high school who borrowed money from me and never paid me back. I should forgive him, but I don't know where he lives. That boss who fired me a couple jobs ago really hurt me. I should forgive him, but we've moved to a different town and he probably doesn't even think he did anything wrong. I've become aware of some things that bother me, but the people who did them have passed away. I need to forgive them too, so you can't always work things out with people you need to forgive.

Eunice: Okay, I see your point, but beware of avoiding the hard work of full forgiveness.

Matt: I don't think I'm avoiding the hard work of forgiving. I'm just trying to be realistic.

Eunice: I do think Jesus wants us to live up to the ideals he taught us.

Matt: So are we to forgive someone continually and repeatedly?

Eunice: Or are we to seek someone's repentance and work out our differences?

Both: Matthew says, "BOTH!"

Week 5

Clothes for the Wedding Banquet

Matthew 22:1-14

Narrator: Matt and Eunice have just finished reading tonight's lesson about the wedding banquet. The gospel of Matthew often seems to be balancing competing emphases; "Matt" and "Eunice" ("Matt" + "hew") represent those differing tendencies.

Eunice: Can you imagine not going to a wedding banquet?

Matt: Yes, I can. You know how I hate going to big, fancy parties. Don't you remember your cousin's wedding last summer?

Eunice: Yes, I do remember. What about it?

Matt: Well, many of your family didn't attend.

Eunice: That was different. The bride had this big feud with her parents about whom to invite and that caused a bunch of hurt feelings, so people boycotted the wedding reception.

Matt: That's what I mean — I can imagine not going to a wedding reception just like some of your family.

Eunice: But what if you lived in England and you received an invitation to a wedding banquet like the one for Prince William and Kate's wedding a few years ago. Would you really not go?

Matt: In that case, I suppose I would go. It would almost be my duty as a loyal citizen. Besides, I imagine the food and drink would be high-class and plentiful.

Eunice: Yes, it would be your duty. That's what is puzzling about this parable. The invited guests who weren't willing to come to the feast were not being faithful to their king, and their refusal to come would be seen as shaming the king. It was almost an act of rebellion. That's why it's difficult for me to imagine the invited guests refusing to attend the banquet.

Matt: That is puzzling, but the king made up for it by filling up the tables with others who were willing to come. No sense in wasting all that good food!

Eunice: Do you think the king would care about wasting food? I thought it was really generous of him to welcome all kinds of people — good and bad — to his banquet. There must have been people there that you would not expect kings to associate with.

Matt: Yes, generous and even surprising. Just like it would be not only generous but also quite surprising if I received an invitation to a wedding of British royalty.

Eunice: Right! I did say "if you lived in England." But that brings me to something else that puzzles me. If the king was so generous, why did he throw out the guest without a wedding garment?

Matt: Wouldn't you dress up to go to a wedding banquet?

Eunice: Where was this poor person supposed to get special wedding clothes?

Matt: Even poor people have some good clothes set aside for special occasions, or he could have borrowed something from neighbors.

Eunice: But it sounds like they were dragged in off the streets. He wouldn't have had time to go back home and change clothes.

Matt: Maybe the king had racks of wedding garments hanging up in the banquet hall that all the guests could pick from. Why wouldn't you put on some of these good clothes?

Eunice: I don't know. Maybe nothing fit him right. If what the king wanted was to have guests at the tables for the wedding feast, why would he care about what they wore?

Matt: Maybe he not only wanted guests at his table; maybe he also wanted the guests to honor and respect him.

Eunice: If this were just a quirky story about some eccentric king it wouldn't matter, but I'm assuming that the king in the story is supposed to represent God. It seems to me that the king's sending out his slaves to bring in all kinds of people, good and bad, is a sign of God's unconditional love. The end of the story seems to contradict that.

Matt: Do you think that God's love is unconditional?

Eunice: Yes, don't you? God loves the whole world, and you don't have to do anything to earn it. Didn't you learn that in Confirmation class?

Matt: Yes, I did, but I still think that God's love is conditional.

Eunice: How can you say that? God's love is given freely to all.

Matt: Actually, I agree with that, but I also think that God expects a response. God expects us to respond in love and obedience.

Eunice: So we have to *earn* God's love by obeying God?

Matt: No, we can't earn God's love; it is a free gift. But if we realize how great that gift is, we cannot help but honor God and love others in response.

Eunice: Somehow it doesn't seem right to place conditions on God's love, but I agree that God's love for us demands a response.

Matt: See! That's what I mean!

Eunice: Don't be so smug! I must have given in too quickly. I can see that God expects us to respond to God's love, but that's not the same as placing conditions on that love.

Matt: It's not?

Eunice: No. Placing conditions on God's love means that God won't love us unless we do something.

Matt: I think it's different than that. God wants a relationship with us and assumes that there's a give and take in this relationship. God offers love; a genuine relationship of love will result in a loving response on our part. Hey, does your mother love you?

Eunice: What kind of question is that? Of course she does!

Matt: Well, I can imagine that you might be difficult to love.

Eunice: Thanks a lot!

Matt: Okay, so your mother loves you. Is that condi-

	tional or unconditional?
Eunice:	She loves me unconditionally!
Matt:	Hmmm, really? Didn't she ever expect things of you — like cleaning your room, helping with meals, or remembering her birthday?
Eunice:	Yes, but she would still love me if I forgot.
Matt:	Right, but her loving relationship still had expectations.
Eunice:	I like "expectations" better than "conditions."
Matt:	Whatever word we use, a loving relationship means love flowing back and forth.
Eunice:	God's love comes to us freely —
Matt:	— and then we love in response, doing loving things that God expects.
Eunice:	So the wedding guest's problem is that he didn't show his appreciation for the king's generosity by wearing the clothes the king expected?
Matt:	Yes.
Eunice:	Okay, I guess. I would feel better if I knew that the king provided the clothes he expected.
Matt:	Perhaps — but how did everyone else get the clothes they needed? Maybe they appreciated the king's generosity and this man didn't.
Eunice:	So — is God's love unconditional?
Matt:	Or is God's love conditional?
Both:	Matthew says, "Both!"

www.ingramcontent.com/pod-product-compliance
Lightning Source LLC
Chambersburg PA
CBHW060211050426
42446CB00013B/3052